William Gustavus Whiteley

The Revolutionary Soldiers of Delaware

Vol. 1

William Gustavus Whiteley

The Revolutionary Soldiers of Delaware
Vol. 1

ISBN/EAN: 9783337307462

Printed in Europe, USA, Canada, Australia, Japan

Cover: Foto ©ninafisch / pixelio.de

More available books at **www.hansebooks.com**

THE

REVOLUTIONARY SOLDIERS

OF

DELAWARE.

A PAPER

READ BY

WILLIAM G. WHITELEY, ESQ.,

BEFORE THE TWO HOUSES OF THE DELAWARE LEGISLATURE,

February 15th, 1875.

PRINTED BY ORDER OF THE LEGISLATURE.

WILMINGTON, DELAWARE:
JAMES & WEBB, PRINTERS,
1875.

The following paper was prepared for and read before the Historical Society of Delaware ; and was afterwards, by request, read before the Legislature.

For many of the facts and incidents stated, it is proper to say that the writer is indebted to " The Life of George Read," by William T. Read, Esq. ; the various lives of General Greene ; " Huffington's Delaware Register," and " Lee's Memoirs."

THE

REVOLUTIONARY SOLDIERS

OF DELAWARE.

———∘∘⫯∘∘———

GENTLEMEN OF THE
  SENATE AND HOUSE OF REPRESENTATIVES :

I feel confident that you will not consider it pedantic if I
begin this paper with an extract from Sallust :—who says, in
his history of the Jugurthine war :

"Sæpe audivi, Q. Maximum, P. Scipio, prætorea civitatis nostræ præ-
claros viros, solitos ita dicere, cum majorum imagines intuerentur, vehe-
mentissime sibi animum ad virtutem accendi. Scilicet non ceram illam,
neque figuram tantam vim in sese habere ; sed memoria rerum gestarum
eam flammam egregiis viris in pectore crescere, neque prius sedari, quam
virtus eorum famam atque gloriam adæquaverit.

"Often have I heard that Quintus Maximus, Publius Scipio, and other
renowned men of our commonwealth, used to say, that whenever they beheld
the images of their ancestors, they felt their minds greatly excited to virtue.
It could not be the wax or the marble which possessed this power, but the
recollection of their great actions kindled a generous flame in their breasts,
not to be quelled, till they also by valor had acquired equal fame and glory."

It is not so much to excite a spirit of emulation of the deeds of *our* ancestors, that I have consented to read before your Bodies, a paper on "The Revolutionary Soldiers of Delaware," as it is to do something, however little, to prevent their deeds from being forgotten. Both as a State, and as individuals we have been very negligent of the collection and preservation of the facts relating to the part our State took in the Revolution. Whatever the State had in the way of Journals of the colonial legislature, were in manuscript, and many of them have been lost ; and but few of the original rolls and other returns of the regiments are in the Secretary of State's office.

We have had, several attempts to give a history of our regiments, but it was in every case imperfect and often erroneous ; it could not and cannot well be otherwise ; the data being so insufficient and unsatisfactory. This is to be regretted ; for we, of Delaware, have great and just cause to be proud of the acts, conduct and heroism of our Revolutionary Soldiers. In less than a month after the declaration of Independence we had eight hundred men in the field ; who fought at Brooklyn, White Plains, Trenton and Princeton ; and by April of 1777, we had another regiment of like number ; who fought at Brandywine, Germantown, Monmouth, Camden— twice at Camden, Cowpens, Guilford, Ninety-six, and at Eutaw ; and this latter one never laid down its arms, though reduced almost to a corporal's guard, until Cornwallis laid down his arms at Yorktown, and Leslie evacuated Charleston. In fact there was not a battle during the Revolution worthy of name, except the Battles of Bunker Hill and Yorktown, in which one of the " Delaware Regiments" did not participate. And in the latter, though Hall's Regiment itself, or rather what was left of it, was not present, it being at that time with Greene in the Carolinas, seven hundred recruits raised in Maryland and Delaware for Smallwood's and Kirkwood's regiments, were stopped on their march to join their respective regiments, and ordered to join the army before Yorktown : and in this way the regiment itself may be said to have participated also in the siege and battle of Yorktown—the decisive battle of the war.

Our population, at the outbreak of the Revolution, being only 37,500, the number of troops we could furnish could not be very large, and yet, by the second year of the war, we furnished and sent to the front, three Regiments, viz : Col. Haslet's, Col. Patterson's and Col. Hall's, and a partisan Company, Capt. Allen McLane's.

Haslet's Regiment, as will be hereafter seen, remained in the army only up to the battle of Princeton.

Patterson's was a part of the "Flying Camp," as it was called, a body of men called out for temporary duty, which will also be explained hereafter. They were both *State* troops ; that is, troops organized under our Colonial laws, and furnished by the colony or State of Delaware, upon the call of the Congress, who appointed their field officers. The Regiment of Col. Hall was the only "Continental" one we furnished. "Continental," because it was organized under a law of the Continental Congress, and this is the Regiment referred to, when we speak of the "Delaware Regiment."

I shall write of the three in their order.

Col. Henry Neall had, in the latter part of the war, a Regiment called the Second Delaware Battalion, but I do not find that it was in any battle.

Before I refer to Haslet's Regiment and its officers—the first Regiment raised—raised in fact before the Declaration of Independence, and participating in the battle of Brooklyn, or Long Island in less than a month after it marched from Dover, permit me to refer to the feeling in our State in reference to the war of the Revolution. Whilst a majority of our people were undoubtedly friendly and favorable to it, there were a great many who were honestly opposed to an appeal to arms against the mother country. Some took this view from a conviction that the evils complained of were trifling ; some, that though the wrongs were great, Great Britain, upon a fair representation being made of them, would at once redress them ; some, conscientiously believed their allegiance to be due to the Government under which they were born, and refused to throw it off ; and others, I am constrained to say, though few in numbers, were actuated by fear, and a desire to protect their persons and property. The views and positions taken by the first three classes, viz, those who thought the evils trifling ; those who thought the mother country would redress them without an appeal to arms ; and those who refused to throw off their allegiance ; are not to be wondered at, when we consider their descent, which was purely English. The people of Kent and Sussex especially were so ; there was with them no intermixture of other nations ; there had been with them but very few Irish, fewer Scotch, and absolutely none from the Continental nations ; they were also a peculiarly isolated people ; off of the routes of what little traveling was done in those days, few of them, besides their merchants, ever visiting Philadelphia, Wilmington or Baltimore ; an agricultural, and, of course, a conservative people, not disposed to change their views without due deliberation, and for weighty reasons, they both lived and clothed themselves from off of their farms : they paid no taxes upon anything, especially not upon their *tea*, for *their* tea was made from the root of the sassafras.   It is not, therefore, surprising that these people for awhile hung back, and did not unite zealously and ardently in the cause of the Colonies ; that they should require some *electioneering*, some personal influence, some arguments to be brought to bear upon them.   There was a man, however, to do this, and who did it, and nearly all of our people holding these views became, in a short time, under his persuasive eloquence, *ardent Whigs*.   That man was Cæsar Rodney. Let us see what he did, ably seconded, of course, by George Read and Thomas McKean, his colleagues in the Continental Congress.   Upon the 7th of June, 1776, Richard Henry Lee, of Virginia, introduced his justly celebrated resolution " that the United Colonies are, and of right ought to be, free and independent States ; and that the political connection between them and Great Britain is, and ought to be, totally dissolved."

This resolution was debated on the 8th and 10th days of June by Congress in committee of the whole, but, as Mr. Jefferson says in his memoirs, " it appearing that New York, Pennsylvania, *Delaware* and Maryland were not yet matured for falling from the *parent stem*, but were rapidly maturing to that state, it was thought prudent to wait awhile for them, and to postpone the final decision until July the first." The resolutions of our General Assembly, passed March 22d, 1776, instructing our deputies in Congress, did not authorize them to vote for independence, but enjoined on them to "embrace every favorable opportunity to effect a reconciliation with Great Britain."

Upon the postponement of the debate on Lee's resolution, Rodney immediately started for Dover, and chiefly through his influence, the General Assembly, then in session, passed unanimously, on the 14th of June A. D. 1776, new instructions to our deputies in Congress, authorizing them "to concur with the other delegates in Congress, in adopting such measures as shall be judged necessary for promoting the liberty, the safety and interests of America, &c., &c." Under these instructions our whole delegation signed the Declaration of Independence. But Rodney's influence had been at work before this. Spending a few days in Congress, which, as you know, sat in Philadelphia, he would suddenly leave that city, at night, and drive to Dover, from there to Sussex, haranguing, talking, imploring, until, by the time the General Assembly met in June, 1776, he had talked the people up to the separating point ; he had ripened the fruit until it fell "from the parent stem," and, I think, *to him*, more than to any other man in Delaware, do we owe the position which our State and people took in that, to us and to the world, most important contest. John Adams, in his diary, thus describes him : "Cæsar Rodney is the oddest looking man in the world : He is tall, thin and slender, and pale ; his face is not bigger than a large apple, yet, there is sense, and fire, spirit, wit and humor in his countenance."

But there was a class of our people whom even Rodney could not influence, and who constituted the "Delaware Tories." They were those who thought it for *their interest*, "better for the safety of their persons and property," to be loyalists. They argued that this Peninsula had an extensive border ; on the Delaware side bounded by the Delaware Bay and Atlantic Ocean ; on the Maryland side by the Chesapeake Bay; that it was thus open to the incursions of a powerful enemy, whose fleets surrounded it on every side, and it was not safe to render themselves obnoxious to a power who could at any time seize upon their persons and property. These people, though few, had their influence ; their appeals were to the strongest motives actuating humanity, to wit : the safety of life, and limb, and property. But as we have seen, a large majority of our people resisted them, how nobly and bravely, let Rodney say. In a letter written by him during the struggle, he says :

"He that dare acknowledge himself a Whig, near the waters of the Delaware, where not only his property, but his person, is every hour in danger of being carried off, is more, in my opinion, to be depended upon, than a *dozen Whigs* in security."

But to the history of Haslet's regiment.

Before the Declaration of Independence a regiment had been raised by Col. John Haslet, and mustered into the state's service ; it was composed of eight companies and numbered eight hundred men. Its officers were appointed by the Congress, upon recommendations made by the Council of Safety of the " Three Lower Counties of Delaware." That is, the Council recommended to Congress the names of several persons for Colonel, Lieutenant Colonel, and Major, from whom the Congress elected by ballot, these various officers. Upon January 19th, 1776, this election was proceeded with ; and, as the Journals of Congress say, "the ballots being taken, John Haslet, Esquire, was elected Colonel ; Gunning Bedford, Esquire, Lieutenant Colonel ; and John Macpherson, Esquire, Major." But Macpherson was *dead* before he was *elected*. He was, as will be seen hereafter, an aid to General Montgomery, and was killed along side of his General in the storming of Quebec, December 31st, 1775 ; the intelligence of his death not having been received on January 19th, 1776, when he was elected Major. But this intelligence reaching the Delaware Assembly sometime in March, this entry is found in the Journals of Congress.

" The Assembly of the Counties on Delaware, having recommended a gentleman to be Major of the Battalion ordered to be raised in those Counties in the room of John Macpherson, who fell before Quebec, and never received his commission ; the Congress proceeded to the election, and the ballots being taken and examined, Thomas McDonough was elected, March 22d, 1776."

The officers of the regiment were

Colonel, John Haslet.

Lieutenant Colonel, Gunning Bedford.

Major, Thomas McDonough.

Surgeon, James Tilton.

Chaplain, Joseph Montgomery.

A company consisting of ninety privates, commanded by Captain *Joseph Stidham*, of which *Robert Kirkwood* was first Lieutenant and *Enoch Anderson* Second Lieutenant.

A company consisting of ninety-one privates, commanded by Captain *Nathan Adams ;* of which *James Moore* was First Lieutenant and *James Gordon* Second Lieutenant.

A company consisting of ninety-seven privates, commanded by Captain *Samuel Smith ;* of which *John Dixon* was First Lieutenant and *James McDonough* was Second Lieutenant.

A company consisting of ninety privates, commanded by Captain *Chas. Pope ;* of which *James Wells* was First Lieutenant and *Alexander Stewart* * was Second Lieutenant.

A company consisting of ninety privates, commanded by Captain *Jonathan Caldwell ;* of which *John Patten* was First Lieutenant and *George McCall* was Second Lieutenant.

A company consisting of ninety-three privates, commanded by Captain *Henry Darby ;* of which *Lewis Worrell* was First Lieutenant and *William Popham* was Second Lieutenant.

A company consisting of ninety-one privates, commanded by Captain *Joseph Vaughan ;* of which *Joseph Truitt* was First Lieutenant and *John Perkins* was Second Lieutenant.

A company consisting of ninety-two privates, commanded by Captain *David Hall;* of which *Genethan Harney* * was First Lieutenant and *John Learmouth* was Second Lieutenant.

In a few days after the news of the Declaration of Independence was received at Dover, the regiment marched to the Head Quarters of the army, which was then at New York. I cannot find out precisely when they arrived at Head Quarters, but it could not have been long before the middle of August. They marched from Dover to New York without tents : how provisions were supplied them does not appear, but it is more than probable they supplied themselves along the route. They were brigaded with four Pennsylvania regiments, and Smallwood's Maryland Regiment, and Lord Sterling was the Brigadier. Upon August 27th, 1776, certainly not more than five weeks (one writer puts it three weeks) after marching from Dover, they were in the battle of Brooklyn, or Long Island, as it is sometimes called. And in this battle they behaved with the courage and firmness of veteran soldiers. It was said that the Delawares and Marylanders fought as bravely as men could possibly do. The Marylanders had two hundred and fifty-nine men missing, many of whom were killed. This was owing chiefly to their being separated, by which means the enemy got between them, and obliged them to fight in small parties. But " the Delawares being well-trained, kept and fought in a compact body the whole time, and when obliged to retreat, kept their ranks, and entered the lines in that order, and were obliged, frequently, while retreating, to fight their way through bodies of the enemy."

Cæsar Rodney, in a letter to Thomas Rodney, dated October 2nd, 1776, writing of the battle of Brooklyn, says : (Thomas was his brother, and father of Cæsar A. Rodney.)

" One paragraph of the old man's letter is very full of the great honor obtained by the Delaware Battalion in the affair at Long Island, from the

---

The companies, as I have given them, are not in the order in which they were in the Regiment. "First Company," &c., as the Rolls, which I have found in the Secretary of State's office, do not give their numbers ; neither have I been able to ascertain who was the Adjutant of the Regiment.

* Killed at the battle of Brooklyn.

unparalleled bravery they showed in view of all the Generals and troops within the lines, who alternately praised and pitied them."

This refers to cutting their way, whilst falling back, through bodies of the enemy.

In a subsequent letter to the same, he says :

"The Delaware and Maryland Regiments stood firm to the last; they stood for four hours drawn up on a hill, in close array, their colors flying, the enemy's artillery playing upon them ; nor did they think of quitting their station until an express order from the General commanded them to retreat;" and closes his letter, after giving the number of killed, wounded and missing, with the remark, "The standard was torn with shot in Ensign Stephens' hands."

The Regiment lost thirty-one in this battle, including two officers, viz : Lieut. Stewart and Lieut. Harney : Major McDonough, Lieut. Anderson and Ensign Course were slightly wounded. It must have been a great disappointment to Col. Haslet, as also to Lieutenant-Colonel Bedford, that they were denied a participation in this battle ; to Haslet particularly ; the Regiment was his pet. He, more than any other man, raised it, and this *its*, and should have been *his*, first battle. But he and Bedford both being members of a General Court Martial, for the trial of a Lieutenant-Colonel Zidwitz, of a New York Regiment, for correspondence with the enemy, were sitting on that Court, in New York, on the day of the fight. But the Regiment was in good hands, those of Major McDonough. Our army retreated after this battle to the city of New York side, and our Regiment being placed in General Mifflin's Brigade, was sent to King's Bridge.

The next general battle in which the Regiment participated, was the battle of White Plains ; then at Trenton on Christmas day, 1776. Here the English lost in killed, wounded and missing, about nine hundred men. I have not been able to obtain any particulars relating to our Regiment in these two battles. They, however, took an efficient part, nine days afterward, in the battle of Princeton, which was fought on January 3d, 1777, and here Col. Haslet was killed while lead-

ing his Regiment gallantly into action. He was charging on
the British lines, about sunrise, and was instantly killed by a
wound through his head, from a rifle-bullet.

John Haslet, who has been truly called the father of his
Regiment, lived at the time of the breaking out of the war at
Dover. He was born in Ireland. He was educated for the
ministry of the Dissenters—Presbyterian—and preached for
some time ; but subsequently studied medicine, and practiced
it with much success in Kent County. He was tall and athletic,
and of generous and ardent feelings, as his birth-place would
indicate. He was a leading Whig, and evidently Cæsar
Rodney's right-hand man ; the one he depended on to get
the people right on the question of Independence, as well as
raising and enlisting soldiers to fight for it. Rodney wrote
him from Congress, daily ; and when Independence was declared, he despatched Ensign Wilson, on the night of the
Fourth of July, on horseback, to carry to Haslet, at Dover, the
news, and the unanimity in our delegation in signing the
Declaration. How Haslet rejoiced, let his answer to Rodney
tell. In reply, on July 6th, he says :

"I congratulate you, Sir, on the important day which restores to every
American his birth-right : a day which every freeman will record with gratitude, and the millions of posterity read with rapture. Ensign Wilson
arrived here last night. A fine turtle feast at Dover anticipated and an-
nounced the declaration of Congress ; even the Barrister himself laid aside
his airs of reserve ; mighty happy."

As the late Mr. William T. Read, of New Castle, remarks
in his life of his father, George Read, " The State of Delaware
has not been unmindful of the services and merits of Colonel
Haslet." In 1777, his remains were deposited in the burying
ground of the First Presbyterian Church, in Philadelphia. In
1783, our Legislature caused a marble slab to be placed over
his grave ; and, in 1841, February 22d, they appointed a committee to superintend the removal of his remains to a vault to
be built in the cemetery of the Presbyterian Church, at Dover,
and authorized them to have a suitable monument, with ap-
propriate inscriptions and devices, prepared and placed over

this, his final resting place. On July 1st, 1841, his remains were disinterred, and conveyed to Dover, escorted by the military of the city of Philadelphia ; and on July 3d, after impressive religious services, and an eloquent address from the Hon. John M. Clayton, they were deposited in the vault prepared for them. The slab placed over his grave in Philadelphia, in 1783, is preserved, by having been made one of the sides of this tomb, and bears this inscription :

In memory of JOHN HASLET, Esquire, Colonel of the Delaware
Regiment, who fell gloriously at the battle of Princeton,
in the cause of American Independence,
January 3d, 1777.
The General Assembly of the State of Delaware, remembering
His virtues as a man,
His merits as a citizen,
and
His services as a soldier,
Have caused this monumental stone, in testimony of their respect,
To be placed over his grave,
MDCCLXXXIII.

The other inscription on the monument is ;

Erected by the State of Delaware,
as a tribute of respect,
to the memory of Colonel JOHN HASLET,
whose remains, according to a resolution of the Legislature,
passed February 22, 1841,
were removed from their resting place,
in the grave-yard of the First Presbyterian Church,
in the city of Philadelphia,
and here re-interred
on Saturday, July 3d, 1841.

Col. Haslet left a son and two daughters. The son, Joseph Haslet, was twice, in 1811 and 1823, elected Governor of this State ; an honor Delaware never conferred upon any other citizen. He was elected, however, under our old Constitution ; under the present one, a Governor elected by the people is ineligible ever afterwards. One of his daughters,

Jemima, married Dr. George Monro, who was a skillful and learned physician, resident in Wilmington, from 1797 until his death in 1820. Of Dr. Monro's children, the only survivor is the present Mrs. Mary A. Boyd, of Wilmington. The other daughter of Col. Haslet married Major Patten, but died childless.

Of the Lieutenant-Colonel ; Gunning Bedford. He was prevented as we have seen, by engagement upon a Court-Martial, from participating in the battle of Long Island. He was with his Regiment, however, in the battle of White Plains, and was there wounded. He was also with it throughout the year 1776, but at the battles of Trenton and Princeton, he was on Washington's staff, as I believe, a volunteer aid.

His Regiment, having been reduced to less than one hundred men at the time of the battle of Princeton, and still lower by that battle, and Haslet, its Colonel, having been killed, was never reorganized, and Bedford retired from the army. After the peace, he was Attorney General of our State ; member of the Legislature ; one of our delegates to the Convention which framed the Constitution of the United States, and was the first Judge of the District Court of the United States ; having been appointed by Washington.

The first Major of this Regiment, though he never joined it, in fact, as I have stated, was dead—killed before Quebec—before he was commissioned, deserves a passing notice. John Macpherson was born in Philadelphia ; studied law, however, in this State, with John Dickinson, and practiced it in New Castle. He was a young man of fine talents, and soon acquired a respectable practice ; and in 1774 upon the resignation of George Read, of the office of Attorney General of the State, he was an applicant for the place, but was not appointed. When the war became inevitable he offered his services to his country, and having become acquainted with General Montgomery, they soon became bosom friends, and he was made by Montgomery his Aid-de-Camp. They were both killed by the same gun, as was Montgomery's other aid, Cheeseman. As the last of the British soldiers fled from the

Battery, Montgomery attacked, they discharged a gun in their flight, and from it, among others, fell these three brave men, and after that, the attack failed. The English officers, forgetting their foes, in the heroes, their adversaries, gathered up their breathless remains, and committed them to kindred earth, with pious hands and honors meet.

Thomas McDonough, elected, as we have seen, Major in place of Macpherson, was a physician, living and practicing his profession at the village, now called for him, in St. George's Hundred, in New Castle county. He did not remain in the service after the battle of Princeton. Upon Haslet's death the Regiment was disbanded. A great many of its officers having obtained commissions in Hall's Regiment, joined it, or had joined it, before the battle of Princeton. Major McDonough returned to private life and to his profession. He was the father of Commodore Thomas McDonough, celebrated in the last war with England, as the victor in the battle of Lake Champlain.

The army under Washington being, in the summer and fall of 1776, occupied in the defence of New York, the shores of New Jersey, of Pennsylvania, Delaware and Maryland were open to the British, who, disembarking their troops anywhere along these shores, could march them not only into the very heart of the confederacy, but could take our army in the rear. Congress, therefore, called on New Jersey, Delaware and Maryland, to raise, equip and march ten thousand men to form a " flying camp," to protect the Middle Colonies, and to serve until December 1st, 1776.

The Battalion called for, furnished by Delaware, was placed under the command of Col. Samuel Patterson. He owned a grist mill on the Christiana, above the village of Christiana, (now Smalley's mill) and carried on the business of a miller there. He also as appears by his epitaph upon his tomb in the Presbyterian Church yard, at Christiana, was a Brigadier General of our State Militia.

He does not appear to have had a happy time with his troops, but it was not his fault. The mode and terms of enlistment, the manner in which the officers were chosen, &c.,

all was fatal to everything like discipline. After he got them to Philadelphia about one-half of them laid down their arms, and swore they would not go, without the same bounty that the Pennsylvania troops received. He succeeded, however, in getting most of them off, by threatening to send for two battalions of other troops and having them all disarmed and arrested. In a letter to George Read, written from Philadelphia, September 19th, 1776, in giving an account of his trouble, as above, in getting his men to march, he says :

"I at last got them down to the wharf, fixed bayonets at the head of it, and sent them off. Capt. Woodgate's arms not being done, I kept his Company to go with me, but this morning I learned, to my astonishment, that his whole Company, save eleven men, had deserted during the night,"

And then adds,

"I shall give you a small opinion on Battalion affairs. If ever you order one other, never sacrifice liberty to licentiousness, by leaving the officers to be chosen as mine were. Had I known the men in general, I would not have went with them. Some few excessive good, others, perhaps, another day may be brave, not at present. In my opinion, they had better have staid at home."

In another letter to the same, of the date of September 22d, 1776, from New Brunswick, he tells Mr. Read to have all the deserters arrested, and not to suffer them to pilfer the public money and all arms and accoutrements.

In another letter of October 4, 1776, from Amboy, he appears in rather better humor, except with the Kent and Sussex levies. He says, he has four hundred and sixty-one men, rank and file. But adds :

" If ever I come campaigning again, I should never be for bringing up the men from *below*. They are not fit for *fatigue*, *have no constitutions, and are always dissatisfied*. Almost fifty or sixty of them every day sick and unfit for duty, and fond of desertion, as you have seen at Philadelphia."

However, in a postscript, he adds :

" Since they left Philadelphia, the Battalion is sorry for their misbehavior. It was owing to a rascal telling them they were fools to go without their bounty."

The Colonel was mistaken in his estimate of the lower County troops ; his anger and worriment at the conduct of some of them biased his judgment. Of this no other proof need be adduced than that, at least one-half, if not more, of both Haslet's and Hall's Regiments were from the counties of Kent and Sussex, and no men fought better, or withstood more fatigue ; and the gallant Captain Caldwell and his Company, from whom our soldiers derived the name of " Blue Hen's Chickens," were from Kent County.

Patterson himself got improved in his humor and estimate of his men later along. On November 4th, in writing to Read, he says :

" I have some noble officers in my Battalion, whom I could recommend, if a door open,"

and in the only skirmish they had with the British, speaks highly of the conduct of his men.

The truth is that it was not alone in Patterson's Regiment that there was dissatisfaction, that it was not receiving a bounty equal to the Pennsylvania troops, which caused such mutinous conduct. There was, in the latter part of 1776 and early part of 1777, great difficulty in getting troops throughout all the Colonies. It was not alone in Delaware. Whether the opinion was becoming fixed, that we would fail, that Great Britain would conquer us, I know not. But such was the fact. One thing, I think the Congress relied too much on the militia. Troops should have been raised by volunteers, under calls upon the Colonies, and the troops thus raised engrafted on, or added to, the Continental army. Mr. Joseph Henry Rogers, of New Castle, has in his possession a roll, and the answers of the men, whom the then Sheriff of this County, John Clark, Esq., was endeavoring to enroll in a Militia Company, in the early part of 1777, for recruits for the Flying Camp.

2

Names.	Answers.
Slator Clay,	Will not march.
Richard Janvier,	Will not march.
John Powell,	Ready and willing to march.
David Morton,	Same.
George Read,	Same.
Thomas Cooch, Jr.,	Same.
Robert Wiley,	I'm damned if I march.
Edward Sweeny,	Family in distress.
James Wilson,	Hired one in his place.
John Booth, Jr..	Substitute in Continental Army.
Joseph Tatlow,	Will not march.
Daniel Smith,	Son in his place.
James Faith,	Will not march.
William Hazlett,	I never will march.
Thomas Nodes,	I'm damned if I march.

And so their answers went. Sick, absent, " will not march," &c., that out of a Company of sixty-three men only twenty-two proffered themselves ready and willing to march.

The officers of the " Flying Camp" were :

> Samuel Patterson, Colonel.
> George Latimer,* Lieut. Colonel.
> William Moody,† Captain.
> Joseph Caldwell, Captain.
> Thomas Kean,‡ Captain.
> James Dunn, Captain.
> Thomas Skillington, Captain.
> Matt. Manlove, Captain.
> John Woodgate, Captain.
> Nathaniel Mitchell,§ Captain.

The term of enlistment, however, of " The Flying Camp' expired on December 1st, 1776 ; winter, at that day, usually com-

---

George Latimer, whom I take to be the brother of Dr. Henry Latimer, a Surgeon of the Revolution, is thus spoken of in a letter from a British spy:—"At Newport is the habitation and effects of one of McKinley's Privy Council, a vile rebel, well known by the name of George Latimer—his father a Judge of Common Pleas."

† Captain Moody was the father of John Moody, some years since a Sheriff of New Castle County.

‡ Captain Thomas Kean was the father of the late Matthew Kean of Wilmington.

§ Nathaniel Mitchell was from Sussex County, and in 1805 elected Governor of the State.

mencing by that time, which was protection enough both to the
Middle Colonies and Washington's rear ; and the soldiers com-
posing the camp returned to their homes, much to their own
pleasure and doubtless the same to their commander. Congress had, by the fall of 1776, become enlightened on the subject of militia, and short terms of enlistment. The troubles and
dissatisfaction in what might be called the regular army, as
well as in " The Flying Camp," demonstrated, that if success
was to be obtained, the army must be reorganized. And,
therefore, on September 16th, 1776, Congress resolved " that
eighty-eight Battalions be enlisted as soon as possible, to
serve during the present war, and that each State furnish
their respective quotas in the following proportions." Without giving them at length, it is only necessary to say, that
Delaware's quota was one Battalion—a Battalion in Revolutionary times meant eight hundred men. The resolution of
Congress gave the very small bounty of twenty dollars to
non-commissioned officers and privates, and one hundred
acres of land to those who served during the war, or to their
children, if they were killed, and provided that though the
officers should be commissioned by Congress, their appoint-
ment, except General officers, was to be left to the Government of the several States, and each State must provide
arms, clothing, &c., &c.

This was a step in the right direction, and made the army
what it afterward became, fit, able and capable to compete
with the British soldiers. Let us see what effect it had on
the then army. Haslet's Regiment will serve for an illustra-
tion. He had left Dover in July with eight hundred men, not
precisely militia, but our State troops, as they were called. It
is true they had gone through the battles of Brooklyn and
White Plains, but those could not have depleted it to the
number I now state. In a general return of the army in service on November 3, 1776, Haslet's Delaware Regiment is
returned as follows :

One Colonel; one Lieutenant-Colonel; three Captains ; not a single
First Lieutenant ; three Second Lieutenants ; five Ensigns ; one Chaplain;

one Adjutant, and one Mate; twelve Sergeants; nine Drummers and Fifers; two hundred and seventy-three privates; twenty-six sick and present, and two hundred and twenty-eight sick and absent—which meant at home—a total of only five hundred and forty eight. of which, officers included, of those present and fit for duty, about three hundred.

The same general return was made on December 22nd, following—three days before the battle of Trenton, and we find this state of things. Present and fit for duty:—One Colonel ; One Lieutenant-Colonel ; One First Lieutenant ; Not a single Second Lieutenant ; Two Ensigns ; One Adjutant ; One Mate ; Five Sergeants ; One Drummer and Fifer ; and ninety-two privates ; Thirty-two present and sick ; a grand total of only one hundred and twenty-four, and all that constituted Haslet's Regiment in the battles of Trenton and Princeton ! Where were the officers, you will ask ; and where were the privates ? Delaware had been called on for her quota under this resolution of Congress ; the men to serve during the War was the attraction, and Haslet's officers left him to get positions in the new regiment. Of Haslet's officers, Captain David Hall became Colonel of this new regiment ; Captain Charles Pope, its Lieutenant Colonel ; Captain Joseph Vaughan, its Major ; Lieutenant John Patten, a Captain ; Lieutenant Robert Kirkwood a Captain ; Lieutenant Anderson, a Lieutenant ; Ensign Peter Jaquett, a Captain ; Lieutenant Learmonth, a Captain, and Lieutenant James Moore a Captain. Thus nine officers from Haslet's Regiment obtained appointments in Colonel David Hall's new Regiment. These officers doubtless carried off a great many of their men. No wonder, therefore, that on the 3rd of November and on the 22nd of December Haslet made such a poor show in his return of both officers and men. He himself had evidently become disgusted and chagrined ; there was found in his pocket when he was killed, an order permitting him to return home to recruit for his Regiment.

This regiment of Hall's became the justly celebrated "Delaware Regiment." The first company to join it was Captain John Patten's. They were mustered in on November 30th, 1776. The second company was Captain Robert Kirkwood's, mustered in on the next day, December 1st, 1776. The commissions of these two as Captains, bore these respective dates : Patten's, November 30th, and Kirkwood's, December 1st, 1776.

As these two companies were the pioneers of the Regiment, I will give the names of their officers.

FIRST, PATTEN'S.

Captain, John Patten.
Lieutenant, William McKennan.
Ensign, Elijah Skillington.
First Sergeant, William Maxwell.
Second Sergeant, Archibald McBride.
First Corporal, Henry Rowan.
Second Corporal, David Young.
Third Corporal, Dennis Dempsey.

Privates, thirty-two.

KIRKWOOD'S WAS,

Captain, Robert Kirkwood.
Lieutenant, Richard Wilds.
Ensign, Griffith Jordan.
Sergeants, Daniel Cochran.
"   James Dougherty.
"   Samuel Davis.
"   Robert Hewes.
Corporals, James Stenson.
"   Moses Joab.
"   James Lowery.
"   Archibald McBride.
And twenty-two Privates.

These and the other six companies, which afterward joined the Regiment, were filled up to the standard, during the winter and following spring. By the Journals of our Colonial Legislature, it appears there was the usual difficulties and delays in filling up the Regiment, clothing and arming it. But by the beginning of April, all was completed, and the officers appointed.

They were as follows :

> Colonel, David Hall.
> Lieut. Colonel, Charles Pope.
> Major, Joseph Vaughan.
> Adjutant, George Purvis.
> Pay Master, Edward Roche.
> Quarter Master, Thomas Anderson.
> Surgeon, Reuben Gilder.
> Surgeon's Mate, John Platt.

Their commissions bear date April 5th, 1777.

It is very difficult to obtain a correct history of the regiment for the years 1777-8—9. What we have is from tradition, and the private letters and papers of its officers, and these last are very few and difficult to find ; the descendants of those officers apparently caring nothing for their preservation, and those who have had the charge of the papers of the State have been equally negligent and careless of the preservation of the rolls, returns, and other records relating and belonging to the regiment. There are in the State House at Dover, but few original rolls, or other returns, or papers of any kind, of the regiment.

But we know that the regiment joined Washington in the Jerseys in the spring of 1777, and participated in the Battles of Brandywine, Germantown and Monmouth.

We have, however, no historical account of the particular part or share borne by the Regiment in these battles. Brigades are the smallest bodies of troops mentioned in the returns in Battles of the size of these. But we know that they were not only with Washington in his Battles, but they were with him at Valley Forge, and throughout that long and dreary Winter bore their sufferings and deprivations as became American soldiers.

It was in the South, however, where they won their immortality.

The United States from the beginning of the war had been divided into two military departments, the Northern and Southern : the Southern consisting of the States of Virginia,

North Carolina, South Carolina and Georgia ; all the rest of the States constituted the Northern. In the spring of 1780, the Southern delegates in Congress having for some time before been urging the substitution of a more experienced General in the South, the Congress added Maryland and Delaware to the Southern Department, and ordered General Gates South, as Commander-in-Chief of that Department. And the Maryland and Delaware troops then encamped around Morristown,in New Jersey,were on April 13th, 1780 ordered South. Upon April 16th they took up their line of march. There were two Regiments from Maryland and our one, between 1400 and 1500 men in all. The Baron De Kalb was assigned as their commander. I have not been able to obtain a Roll of the Regiment for the month of April 1780. The companies had become, in the winter of 1779-80 very much reduced, averaging only about thirty-five men ; but by the time of their order to the South, April 13, 1780, they had been recruited up to about sixty men each, making the Regiment about five hundred strong.

I have the rolls of the different companies for February 1780, but have no lists of the recruits. This is owing to the fact that after their march south there are no returns of the Regiment on file in Secretary of State's office.

Muster Roll of the Field, Staff, other officers and privates of the Delaware Regiment of Foot, commanded by Col. David Hall, *for the month of February,* 1780.

Date of Commission.		Rank.
1777, April 5,	David Hall,	Colonel.
1777, April 5,	Charles Pope,	Lieutenant-Colonel.
1777, April 5,	Joseph Vaughan,	Major.
1778, Aug. 15,	George Purvis,	Adjutant.
1778, Sept. 10,	Edward Roche,	Pay Master.
1778, Sept. 10,	Thomas Anderson,	Quarter Master.
1777, April 5,	Reuben Gilder,	Surgeon.
1777, April 5,	John Platt,	Surgeon's Mate.
	FIRST COMPANY.	
1776, Nov. 30,	John Patten,	Captain.
1777, April 5,	Wm. McKennan,	First Lieutenant.
1778, Sept. 8,	Elijah Skillington,	Second Lieutenant.

Non-Commissioned Officers and Privates.

First Sergeant, William Maxwell. Second Sergeant, Archibald McBride.
First Corporal, David Young. Second Corporal, Dennis Dempsey.
Third Corporal, Henry Rowan. Drummer, Benjamin Jones.

Fifer, Joseph Staton.

Privates.

John Clifton,	Samuel Piles,
Patrick McCallister,	Alexander Clark,
Ebenezer Blackshire,	Samuel Dodd,
Patrick Ducy,	Richard Davis,
John Andrews,	Robert Miller,
William Walker,	Frederick Reid,
John Benson,	John McCabe,
Cornelius Hagney,	John McGill,
Thomas McCann,	John Hatfield,
Patrick Burk,	John Robinson,
Levin Leasatt,	Isaac Griffin,
John Barnes,	Michael Dorman,
James Neill,	Robert Dyer,
William Kilty,	James Bennett,
William Newell,	Abraham Mears,
John Mitchell,	Whittinton Clifton,
James Brown,	Hugh Donnelly,

John Highway.

SECOND COMPANY.

1776, Dec. 1,	ROBERT KIRKWOOD,	Captain.
1777, April 5,	DANIEL P. COX,	First Lieutenant,
1778, Sept.	CHARLES KIDD,	Second Lieutenant.

Non-Commissioned Officers and Privates.

First Sergeant, Jonathan Jordan. Second Sergeant, William Seymour.
Third Sergeant, William Reddin. First Corporal, Nehemiah Nichols.
Second Corporal, Christopher Willett. Drummer, Edward Robinson.

Fifer, John Johnson.

Privates.

Adam Johnston,	John Carr,
John McKnight,	William Whitworth,
William Keys,	Henry Willis,
Thomas Townshend,	Eli Dodd,
William Drew,	Stephen Bowen,

John Stuart,
Levi Bright,
James Hammon,
John Miller,
Francis Williams,
Benjamin Bennett,
Stephen Anderson,
John Brown,
James Weighnwright,
Benjamin Thompson,
William Lewis,
John Eirving,

William Donaldson,
Peter Croft.
James Moones,
Cornelius Grimes,
Thomas Toole,
Joseph Preston,
Thomas Walker,
William Heagans,
Joseph Ferguson,
Andrew Bollard,
John Norman,
Joseph Culver.

THIRD COMPANY.

1777, April 5,	JOHN LEARMONTH,	Captain.
1778, Aug. 16,	HENRY DUFF,	First Lieutenant.
1778, Sept. 10,	THOMAS ANDERSON,	Second Lieutenant.

Non-Commissioned Officers and Privates.

First Sergeant,	John Esham.
Second Sergeant,	George Collins.
Third Sergeant,	Seth Brooks.
First Corporal,	Charles Hamilton.
Second Corporal,	William Black.
Drummer,	William Hook.
Fifer,	William Skinner.

Privates.

Michael Lacatt,
Levi Jackson,
James Turner,
Timothy Layfield,
Eliakim Paris,
William Barker,
James Cook,
James Crampton,
George Hill,
Thomas Hollston,
William Lingo,
Jeremiah Brown,
William Hook,
Charles Wharton,
Dennis Flavin,
Jonathan Ireland,

Andrew Dixon,
Mark Beckett,
William Orton,
Thomas Harper,
Charles Connelly,
George Mershaw,
Samuel Latimore,
John Middleton,
William Plowman,
Michael Garvin,
Thomas Harris,
Thomas Flinn,
Henry Neisbett,
Robert Heastings,
Peter Ricords,
David Davis,

John Watkins.

FOURTH COMPANY.

1777, April 5,	PETER JAQUETT,	Captain.
1777, April 5,	JAMES CAMPBELL,	First Lieutenant.
1779, Oct. 27,	STEPHEN McWILLIAM,	Second Lieutenant.

Non-Commissioned Officers and Privates.

First Sergeant,	Mitchell Kershaw.
Second Sergeant,	Mordecai Berry.
Third Sergeant,	Jenkins Evins.
First Corporal,	Michael Elwood.
Second Corporal,	Abijah Houston.
Drummer,	Adam Joland.

Privates.

William Wallis,	Casy Hall,
Isa Williams,	Zadock Tucker,
William Ake,	Thomas Derrick,
John Turner,	Hambleton O'Neall,
William Wright,	John Noble,
James Demar,	Bartholomew Adams,
Michael Dougherty,	Jacob McKinley,
John Joland,	Hugh Fleming,
James Redmand,	William Simpson,
William Jones,	John Cook,
Andrew Daly,	John Gorman,
Johnson Fleetwood,	James Scott,
Matthew Hilford,	John Castle,
Henry Norwood,	Timothy Kilkenny,
William Furbush,	Jacob Benton,
John Gasford,	Robert Stafford,
David Willaby,	John Peoples.

FIFTH COMPANY.

1777, March 1,	JOHN WILSON,	Captain.
1778, Jany. 26,	PAUL QUENSWALT,	First Lieutenant.
1778, Sept. 10,	EDWARD ROCHE,	Second Lieutenant.

Non-Commissioned Officers and Privates.

First Sergeant, Moses Pharis.	Second Sergeant, John Cox.
Third Sergeant, John Spencer.	First Corporal, James Husbands.
Second Corporal, Joseph Emertson.	Third Corporal, John King.

Fifer, Michael Green.

Privates.

Solomon Price,
Robert Downs,
Robert Timmons,
Jesse Timmons,
William Fleming,
William Slay,
Richard Moore,
Nathaniel Norton,
Joshua Brown,
Nathan Arnot,
William Fish,
Samuel Miller.
Samuel Long,
Isaac Carrall,

John Wiley,
John Service,
Elias Meeker,
David Ellis,
Frederick Vanderlip,
Neil Levinston,
Jacob Cork,
John Hill,
Benjamin Moody,
Joseph McAfee,
William Simpson,
Isaac Landsley,
Levin Painter,
Kinley Haslett,

Samuel Wooden.

SIXTH COMPANY.

| 1779, March 1, | JOHN CORSE, | Captain. |
| 1778, Sept. 10, | CALEB BROWN, | First Lieutenant. |

Non-Commissioned Officers and Privates.

First Sergeant, James Murphy.
Third Sergeant, Emanuel Pierson.
Corporal, Charles Dowds.
Fifer, John Jackson.

Second Sergeant, Patrick Dunn.
Corporal, Alexander McDonald.
Corporal, Thomas Miller.
Drummer, William Lewis.

Privates.

Patrick Flinn,
John Todd,
Zedekiah Ridgway,
Littleton Pickron,
William Burch,
James Wilkinson,
John Conner,
John Hill,
William Stanton,
James Marsh,
Harmon Clark,
Purnell Truitt,
Edward Hallowell,

William Legg,
Jasper Muscord,
Thomas Rhodes,
Richard Taylor,
Anthony Delavonia,
John King,
William Dixon,
John Furbis,
John Stewart,
William Perry,
John Patterson,
Roger McCormick,
John Harris,

James Carson,
Moses Niells,
John Blake,
George Lea,

John Bently,
William Grave,
Samuel Bass,
Edward Morris.

SEVENTH COMPANY.

| 1776, Dec. 4, | JOHN RHODES, | Captain. |
| 1778, Aug. 16, | CALEB P. BENNETT, | First Lieutenant. |

Non-Commissioned Officers and Privates.

First Sergeant, Hosea Wilson.
First Corporal, Samuel Cross.
Drummer, Robert Thompson.

Second Sergeant, Charles Coulter.
Second Corporal, Thomas Nash.
Fifer, William Baily.

Privates.

William Smith,
William Willis,
Patrick Coleman,
Edward Conner,
William Murphey,
Thomas Saxon,
Thomas Collins,
Jacob Cook,
Richard Hudson,
Joshua Shehorn,
John Hurbert,
Christopher Crook,
John Neilson,
John Cornell,

Richard Pierson,
Patten Burris,
George Clifton,
Neill McCann,
William Kelty,
Samuel Nicholas,
Martemas Sipple,
John Pemberton,
Daniel Lawler,
Richard Curryfoot,
John Preston,
Richard Harris,
William Holt,
John McConaughey,

Richard Coffill.

EIGHTH COMPANY.

| 1777, Oct. 15, | GEORGE PURVIS, | Captain. |
| 1778, Aug. 16, | JOSEPH HOSMAN, | First Lieutenant. |

Non-Commissioned Officers and Privates.

Second Lieutenant, Joseph Hosman.
Second Sergeant Thomas McGuire.
First Corporal, Jacob Finly.
Third Corporal, James Corse.

First Sergeant, John Kowan.
Third Sergeant, Thomas Thompson.
Second Corporal, Dennis Leary.
Drummer, David Miller.

Fifer, John Hackney.

Privates.

Jonathan Coote,	Nathan Bowen,
Ellis Flower,	William Peirson,
Alexander Dunlap,	Patrick McCurdy,
Daniel Handley,	Joseph Tapp,
Alexander Flower,	Zadock Morris,
Patrick Mooney,	John Randorn,
John Lahcat,	William Roe,
Frederic Holden,	John Phillips,
John Duffy,	Thomas Mason,
John Cullen,	Thomas Mattingly,
Jesse Royall,	Daniel Daily,
John Purneill,	William Oglesby,
William Gattery,	Daniel Murray,
James Bersine,	James Kennig,
Charles Freeman,	John Stephens,
Levin Hicks,	Thomas Gordan,
Thomas Clark.	Thomas Townsend.

John Cazier, Sergeant Major.
Robert Oram, Second Sergeant Major.
Herdman Anderson, Drum Major.
Timothy Cook, Fife Major.

Col. Hall did not march with his regiment, nor did he ever join it again. Having been seriously wounded at Germantown, he had not recovered from it sufficiently to warrant his taking the field. Lieutenant-Colonel Pope was on furlough at the time of the march, and did not go South.

They marched from Morristown to the Head of Elk, as it was called, now Elkton, in Cecil County, Maryland. This march was through Philadelphia and Wilmington—the distance being 108 miles. They were veterans of three years' service, as thoroughly trained, as brave and as good soldiers as the Continental Army could turn out, and if Greene had only been assigned *at that time* to the command of the Southern Department instead of Gates, their worse than decimation at Camden would have been avoided, and the lives of many of these noble and glorious men saved. A description of their appearance as they passed through Philadelphia on this march will be interesting. It is in a letter from a lady :

"What an army, said both Whig and Tory, as they saw them pass. The shorter men of each company in the front rank, the taller men behind them—some in hunting shirts—some in uniforms—some in common clothes —some with their hats cocked, and some without, and those who did cock them, not all wearing them the same way, but each man with a green sprig, emblem of hope, in his hat, and each bearing his firelock with what, even to uninstructed eyes, had the air of skillful training."

From the Head of Elk all the troops were taken by water to Petersburg, in Virginia, except the Park of artillery, which went by land, guarded by a detachment from all the line. In the short description of the march, and of the state of the troops on it, and their want of provisions, I extract freely from a manuscript "Journal of the Southern expedition, by William Seymour, a Sergeant Major of the Delaware Regiment," which Journal is now in the possession of the Historical Society of Pennsylvania. Seymour says that the troops having all met at Petersburg on the 26th of May—remaining there four days, then left for Hillsborough in North Carolina, and arrived there on June 22d,—469 miles from Head of Elk. From there they marched to Buffalo Ford, on Deep River, where General Gates took the command. "At this time, says Seymour, we were much distressed for want of provisions— men were sent out to cut the grain, (corn), for daily sustenance—but could scarcely get enough to keep the troops from starving—which caused many of the men to desert." A little further on in his journal, in writing of this scarcity, he says :

"That for fourteen days we drew but half pound of flour per man. Sometimes a half pound of beef, but so bad that scarce any mortal could make use of it: and we lived chiefly on green apples and peaches, which rendered us weak and sickly."

George Washington Greene, in the life of his father, Gen. Greene, in describing the sufferings of our troops on this march, for the want of provisions, and whose description corresponds exactly with Seymour's, says, that the officers controlling their hunger, ate only of the lean and unsavory beef which they collected day by day in the woods—that is, they denied themselves the unripe corn, and green apples and green peaches, and adding, some of them made soup out of their beef, and thickening their soup with *hair powder*. Gates had promised them when he took up his line of march from Deep River, "Rum and Rations," " that plentiful supplies were close at hand, and could not fail to reach them in one or at farthest two days." But in this, as in most of his promises in this campaign, he was deceiving his men.

I have nothing to say of his promise of "*rum*," for in Revolutionary times an allowance of it daily was served with the rations.

They were now approaching Camden, the theatre of their first great battle in the South, and where, though the issue was disastrous to the Americans, the Delaware and Maryland troops won imperishable renown. It is not my intention to describe this battle, at least at length ; nor indeed any of the other battles in which they were afterward engaged. To do this, would be foreign from the object of this paper ; all that I shall do will be to recount such parts as our Regiment took in them. The battle of Camden was fought as you all know, on August 16th, 1780. Seymour says under date of 13th, while encamped at Rugely's Mills, thirteen miles from Camden,

"Here we were joined by about three thousand militia from Virginia, and North Carolina, which seemed a good omen of success, but proved to be our utter ruin in the end, for, placing too much confidence in them, they at length deceived us, and left us in the lurch."

In this, as we shall see, Seymour was right. In fact the battle was a mistake ; it was fought by Gates against the advice of his officers, amongst whom conspicuously was De Kalb ; misfortunes of all kinds appeared to centre around them all the preceding night as well as the day of the battle. Seymour says that at midnight on the night of the 15th, just before the order to march, " instead of rum, we were given molasses, which instead of enlivening our spirits, jallop would have been no worse." Then on the march about one o'clock in the morning, the two armies met. They instantly, to use a military phrase, felt each other, and Gates having with a fatuity which was remarkable in this fight, put Armand's

Corps, (which was a made up affair, out of all sorts of material—foreigners, deserters, &c.,) in front.   They no sooner saw the flashes of the enemy's guns, than the whole corps turned its back and ran, carrying confusion and dismay into our ranks. But they not only fled, but robbed in their flight the Baggage Wagons of the Delaware and Maryland Regiments. Both armies now halting until daylight, renewed the fight just at daybreak, *on the part of the Americans*, as Seymour says, " with great alacrity and uncommon bravery," but the Militia, as he has declared, did prove to be their utter ruin.

The veterans of the enemy composed his right, the Virginia Militia our left—here should the Maryland and Delaware Regiments have been, for then it would have been veteran against veteran.

As the enemy drew near, however, the Virginia Militia, some of them firing but once, some of them, without so much as firing a single shot, threw their loaded guns down, and basely retreated ; some, "throwing down their arms and running into the enemy's ranks." The North Carolina Militia soon followed this shameful example. The Continentals, which were the Maryland regiments and our Delaware regiment, not fourteen hundred in all, with a single regiment of North Carolinians, were alone left to oppose the enemy. They stood as men never stood before or since. My words are weighed, and I repeat them, " as men never stood before or since." With three thousand militia flying—tearing through their ranks, "bursting away like an unarmed torrent," with all this demoralization, with Britain's best soldiers pressing them, the flower, it is said, of the British army, commanded by the best of Britain's officers, " they held their ground, charging and repelling charges, broken more than once, and borne down by superior numbers, but forming again and rallying and fighting bravely to the end.   In vain did Otho Williams cry to his men, " Take trees, *men*, choose your trees, men, and give them an Indian charge." In vain did the gigantic DeKalb reform his ranks *when broken*, and lead them to the charge when *reformed*.   In vain did he cry, "Give them the bayonet, men ! give them the bayonet."

In vain did his clear voice ring out cheerily, exhorting, encouraging, guiding, leading, while bullet after bullet struck him with fatal accuracy. What the bayonets of the enemy's foot could not do, the charge of Tarleton's cavalry did ; they broke before it, and what was left of the two Maryland and our Delaware Regiment, retreated. The Delaware Regiment went into this fight five hundred strong. Lee, in his memoirs ; Greene in the life of his father ; Otho Williams in his account of the battle, and our Sergeant Seymour in his diary, all use the same expression, the same language, viz : " In this battle the regiment of Delaware was nearly annihilated," and it was, really and truly. Of the five hundred, there remained after the battle—and remember the battle lasted scarcely an hour —four captains, seven subalterns, three staff officers, nineteen non-commissioned officers, eleven musicians and one hundred and forty-five (145) rank and file, *one hundred and eighty-eight* in all. Eleven commissioned officers and thirty-six privates were made prisoners, forty-seven altogether, making, including prisoners,a total of two hundred and thirty-five, and leaving a dead roll of two hundred and sixty-five for a short fight of one hour. Well might the brave De Kalb, with his dying breath, " breathe benedictions on his faithful brave divisions." Well might he say that it was glorious to die whilst leading such troops. Well might their bravery extort eulogies, as it did, from the enemy ; Cornwallis and Rawdon, and Webster, and even the proud, supercilious, bitter, and cruel soldier, Tarleton, praised them.

So long as they could count on Armand's legion and the Virginia and North Carolina militia, victory appeared certain, for they greatly outnumbered the enemy. Numbers will tell, and they counted on them. But Armand fled before daylight, and the militia with the rising sun. Then De Kalb and Williams, recognizing the emergency, gave their respective orders, the one for an " Indian charge," the other for the " Bayonet." And bravely were these orders obeyed : but decimation followed. Man for man, the result would have been different, but superiority of numbers and Tarleton's cavalry could not be resisted. Otho Williams says they stood too long, but it

3

was in obedience to orders ; they never received orders to retreat nor any order from any General officer from the commencement of the action until it became desperate. Gen. Gates himself was not there to observe the battle, and issue orders accordingly. He had gone off with the flying militia, and upon the evening of the day of the battle, was at Charlotte, sixty miles away. It is not for me to find fault with him, when Gen. Greene and Henry Lee did not. After Saratoga, he can scarcely be accused of cowardice, but he did, in my opinion, at Camden, notwithstanding Charles Lee's warning, " exchange his *Northern* laurels for *Southern* willows."

Among the officers of the Delaware Regiment who were taken prisoners, were Lieutenant-Colonel Vaughan, the commander of the Regiment, and Major Patten. They held the right, and had pressed the enemy back ; but the flight of the militia, relieving that portion of the enemies line in *their* front, the opportunity was seized by him to attack *them* in flank. The capture of these officers shows where the Delaware Regiment was—in the advance. Vaughan starting, as we have seen, with the Regiment from Morristown as its Major, had by reason of Col. Hall's not joining it, become its Lieutenant-Colonel, and Captain John Patten, by reason of being its Senior Captain, became its Major. After their capture these officers were sent to Charleston, and after a detention of some time, were paroled, but not being exchanged, they did not, as they could not, join their Regiment. Their capture put the Regiment under the command of Kirkwood, who became Senior Captain, on Patten's promotion. At Charlotte and Hillsborough he collected what remained of the Regiment, and three companies of Light Infantry being formed out of the different corps, to the command of one of them, composed of the remnants of the Delaware and Second Maryland Regiment, Captain Robert Kirkwood was assigned. They were in all the battles under Greene, in the South, from this time until the surrender of Charleston—Greene, as is well-known, having been sent South to relieve Gates, after the latter's failure at Camden. They were at the Cowpens with Morgan, who told them the night before the battle, " Give them three fires,

Boys, and you are free!" "Yes, the old wagoner will crack his whip over Ben Tarleton in the morning, as sure as you live,"—and he did. But the militia again ran : but this time only to take shelter behind the Continentals. Then it was that the battle was saved, by Colonel Washington's Horse charging and breaking the English Cavalry, and the Delaware and Maryland Light Infantry "giving them the bayonet," under their General, Howard's, order. Seymour in his description in his Diary, of this fight, says :

"Tarleton endeavored to outflank us on the right, to prevent which, Captain Kirkwood wheeled his Company to the right and attacked their left flank so vigorously, that they were soon repulsed ;"

and then goes off into this not very grammatical, but doubtless sincere panegyric of

"Capt. Robert Kirkwood, whose heroick valour and uncommon and undaunted bravery must needs be recorded in history till after years."

In this march to the Cowpens, he also gives this description of the country, the people and their houses ; after speaking of the difficulties of the march, in crossing deep swamps and climbing very steep hills, he says :

" The inhabitants along this way live very poorly ; their plantations, uncultivated, and living in mean houses ; they seem chiefly to be of the offspring of the ancient Irish, being very affable and courteous to strangers."

The regiment was with Greene in his celebrated retreat before Cornwallis from the left bank of the Catawba to the termination of his pursuit of him at Ramsay's Mills. In the management of this retreat, Greene is said to have displayed more of genius, and more of the marks of a great commander than he ever did before or afterward. One of his biographers says :

"Perhaps a brighter era does not adorn the military career of any leader."—Caldwell's Life, p. 250.

It was in the course of *it*, that he turned the current of

adverse fortune, which he afterward directed so that the
enemy were swept from his numerous strongholds in the
southern department, and contributed so pre-eminently to
the speedy and felicitous issue of the war.

Our Sergeant, Seymour, in speaking of this march, says :

"Most of the men were entirely without shoes, and that they marched
night and day, and had no time to cook what provisions they had."

It was on this march that it is related that Greene passing a sentinel who was barefoot, said :

"I fear my good fellow, you must suffer from cold."

"Pretty much so," was the reply. "But I do not complain, for they say in a few days we shall have a fight, and
then, by the blessing of God, I shall take care to secure a pair
of shoes."

The Delawares were with General Greene in the Battle of
Guilford which followed, and which Seymour puts down in his
diary, on the day of the fight, as a drawn battle if not a victory, although Greene fell back.   It was really a victory ;
Greene claimed it, and Cornwallis, after the war was over,
acknowledged it.   Greene in his report of it speaks of the
" *Old* Delaware Company under the *brave* captain Kirkwood, '
and in the same report, in speaking of an attack upon his line
made by Lieutenant-Colonel Webster, of the enemy, (a brave
and gallant officer, who was wounded in making it, and subsequently died) says, after mentioning another flight of the
North Carolina militia :

"Here was posted the first regiment of Maryland, Colonel Gunby—
*   *   the enemy rushed in to close fire, but so firmly was he received by
this body of veterans, supported by Hawes' regiment of Virginia and Kirkwood's company of Delawares, that with equal rapidity he was compelled to
recoil from the shock."

And Henry Lee in his memoirs in describing this battle
says :

"That though the British General fought against two to one, he had greatly the advantage in the quality of his soldiers—General Greene's veteran infantry being only the first regiment of Maryland, *the company of of Delaware under Kirkwood* ("*to whom*, he says in a parenthesis, *none could be superior*) and the legion infantry"—altogether making only 500 rank and file."

They were with Greene at Hobkirk's Hill, or as it is some-times called "the second Battle of Camden." And here Kirkwood, if not assigned the *post* of honor, was assigned to a most responsible position. In detailing his order of Battle, he says :

" Kirkwood with his Light Infantry was placed in front to support the pickets, and retard the enemy's approach. As soon as the pickets began firing, Kirkwood hastened with his light infantry to their support, and the quick, sharp volleys from the woods told how bravely he was bearing up against the weight of the British Army. Still he was slowly forced back, disputing the ground foot by foot, to the hill on which the Americans were waiting the signal to begin. * * * And soon Kirkwood with his light infantry, and Smith with the camp guards and pickets were seen falling slowly back, and pressing close upon them the British van. A few mo-ments more, and Greene and Rawdon stood face to face."

Greene in his orders of the day after the battle uses this language :

" Though the action of yesterday terminated unfavorably to the Ameri-can Arms, the General is happy to assure the troops that is by no means decisive. The extraordinary exertions of the cavalry, commanded by Lieut. Col. Washington, *the gallant behavior of the light infantry commanded by Captain Kirkwood*, and the firmness of the pickets under Captains Benson and Morgan, rendering the advantage expensive to the enemy, highly merit the approbation of the General, and the imitation of the rest of the troops."

Seymour in his diary says :

"In this action the light infantry under Captain Robert Kirkwood were returned many thanks by Gen. Greene *for* their gallant behavior."

Then they were with Greene in the siege of ninety-six. The orders were that Lieutenant Colonel Lee, with the legion of infantry and Kirkwood's Delawares, are ordered to attack on the right : *chosen men and true* they are called in the life of Greene, and nobly did they sustain their character on this day. The assault failed, but Greene felt that he had reason to be proud of his army. In the afternoon orders, he says :

" The General takes great pleasure in acknowledging the high opinion he has of the gallantry of the troops engaged in the attack of the enemy's redoubts. The judicious and alert behavior of the light infantry of the legion, *and those* commanded by Captain Kirkwood, directed by Lieutenant Colonel Lee, met with deserved success, &c., &c."

And then they were with Greene at Eutaw Springs, where, in giving the order of battle, it is said : Washington and Kirkwood closed the rear, forming a reserve of cavalry *and the gallant infantry of Delaware*. In describing a portion of the fight, G. W. Greene, in the life of his father says, after speaking of Washington's attack with his cavalry, the shooting of his horse, and of his being wounded and taken prisoner :

" Kirkwood and Hampton were now at hand, and the men of Delaware pressed forward with the bayonet, while Hampton, collecting the shattered remains of Washington's cavalry, still bleeding but not disheartened, made another trial with them, but the position was too strong to be forced, and *though Kirkwood held his ground*, Hampton was compelled to retire."

And Greene himself, in his letter to the President of Congress, giving a report of this battle, says :

" I think myself principally indebted for the victory obtained, to the free use of the bayonet made by the Virginians and Maylanders, the infantry of the legion, *and Captain Kirkwood's light infantry*, and though few armies ever exhibited equal bravery with ours in general, yet the *conduct and intrepidity of these corps were peculiarly conspicuous*."

This was the last battle in which the regiment was engaged. When the report of it was submitted to Congress by General Greene, they passed a resolution of thanks to him and his army, and included among them is this one :

" That the thanks of the United States in Congress assembled be presented to the officers and men of the Maryland and Virginia brigades, and Delaware battalion of Continental troops, for the unparalleled bravery and heroism by them displayed in advancing to the enemy through an incessant fire, and charging them with an impetuosity and order that could not be resisted."—October 29th, 1781.

This was virtually the end of the war. Cornwallis had surrendered, and there was little if any fighting afterwards : Seymour closes his diary with these words :

"On November 16th, 1782, the Delaware Regiment had orders to hold themselves in readiness to march home from the southward. On the same day started from Head-quarters on the Ashley river for home; coming by way of Camden. Having arrived there November 22nd; were detained thirteen days by orders from General Greene, left on December 5th; coming by way of Salisbury, Petersburgh, Carter's Ferry, on James River, we arrived at Georgetown in Maryland, January 12th, 1783 ; left there the same day and arrived at Christiana Bridge, on the 17th, after a march of seven hundred and twenty miles from Encampment on Ashley River, which was performed with very much difficulty, our men being so very weak after a tedious sickness which prevailed amongst them all last summer and fall."

Before I take leave of Seymour, whose journal is very interesting, and the correctness and truthfulness of which is verified by the reports of others, Greene, Williams, Lee, &c., &c., I must quote a poetic tribute of his to Washington, written in his Journal, and at the end of which his initials, " W. S." are signed.

"O, Washington, thrice glorious name,
    What due rewards can man *dicrie*,
Empires are far below thy aim,
    And sceptres have no charm for thee,
Virtue alone has thy regard,
    And she must be thy great reward."

W. S.

If my object in this paper was an eulogy of the Delaware Regiment, instead of a history of it, and of such of its officers of whom any information can now be gathered, here is the place to stop and make it ; but to do so, would not only be a diversion from the object of this paper, but time would not permit. But I must be permitted to say this, that never before or since is there any record of as many battles in one campaign where the bayonet was so often resorted to—both sides believed in it. Cornwallis doubtless thinking that the half-clothed, barefooted, half-starved rebels could not stand before *it in* the hands of his "Buffs," his "Fusileer's," and his "Guards." But he mistook his men—those ragged, hungry soldiers were as good at it, and feared it less than the British soldiers. Greene, and Williams and Howard believed in it, and Kirkwood knew how to use it. In every battle their cry was, "Give them the bayonet, men, give them the bayonet," and the Delaware Regiment was always one of those selected to *give them the bayonet*.

And again there is scarcely a general order issued by Greene in this whole campaign, after any of his battles, in which the Delaware Regiment is not particularly named as meriting especial praise. This, too, is a most high honor, and considering their almost total and absolute destitution of both clothing and provisions, from the beginning to the ending of the campaign, is remarkable. We have seen how they suffered for provisions in the outset. Throughout the whole campaign, it was but little, if any better.

In clothing, they were worse off, many of them so badly off, that they could not go on parade. Of those who did appear, the ludicrous exhibition of shreds and patches, odds and ends of uniforms and old clothes, made a variety to which no display of a mock military could possibly do justice.

But all these things did not discourage our Continentals. The militia might run away, in battle after battle, as they almost invariably did, *they* only fought the harder. In fact, fighting was what they enlisted for and fighting was what they did. Greene truly described in one of his letters his own and his army's business—"We fight, get beat, rise and fight again." His especial eulogy of his Delaware soldiers, however, was his remark, on his way north, after the war, "that they exceeded all soldiers he had ever seen, as they could fight all day and dance all night."

In Johnson's life of Greene, page 15, (second volume) in describing the battle of Guilford, he says :

"Excepting the Infantry of the legion and Kirkwood's little corps of Delawares, the First Regiment of Marylanders was the only body of men in the American Army who could be compared to the enemy in discipline and experience, and it is with confidence that we challenge the modern world to produce an instance of better service, performed by the same number of men, in the same time."

And here I may remark, that the Company from whom we obtained our sobriquet of " Blue Hen's Chickens" was not in this, Hall's Regiment, as is generally supposed, but in Col. Haslet's. The Company was Captain Jonathan Caldwell's, and was recruited entirely in Kent County. The Blue Hen's brood would have had but small chance of displaying their fighting propensities if they had been taken South, judging from the straits the men were in for want of provisions.

David Hall, the Colonel of this Regiment, was born in Lewes, Sussex County ; was a lawyer by profession, and lived and practiced law at Lewes, at the time he joined Haslet's Regiment. Lewes was then, and up to about the beginning of this century, the county seat of Sussex County. He was quite young when he entered the army. He was with his Regiment up to the battle of Germantown. Here he was severely wounded, and as he did not join his regiment afterward, the inference is, and from what I can gather of his history, the fact was, that it was owing to this wound. He died in 1818, having been in the year 1802 elected Governor of the State. His descendants still reside in Sussex County ; one of them, a grandson—Mr. John W. Walker—in Wilmington.

The first Lieutenant-Colonel was Charles Pope. He lived at Smyrna, and was a merchant. It is to be regretted that so little can be learned as to his history, this is owing probably to his removal with his family, prior to 1800, to Georgia. He continued with his Regiment until 1779, when, as I find by the returns of the Regiment in the Secretary of State's office, at Dover, he came home on furlough, and I cannot find that he ever afterwards joined it.   He certainly did not go South with it.   He is represented to have been a bold, dashing officer.

Major and subsequently Lieutenant Colonel Vaughan lived in or near Bridgeville, in Sussex county.   Unfortunately little is known of his early history.   He was an Englishman, and was engaged in the iron business, and had a furnace near Concord, in Sussex county.   He joined Haslet's Regiment, and in November 1776, held the post of Captain.   Upon the organization of Hall's Regiment he was elected its Major, and held that position until the Regiment was ordered South in April, 1780.   Col. Hall not marching with his regiment, nor the Lieutenant Colonel Pope either, Major Joseph Vaughan was promoted from his Majority to the Lieutenant Colonelcy; he went South with the regiment, but unfortunately, was taken prisoner at Camden, and not having been exchanged, was never with it afterwards.   All the reports we have name him as a brave and efficient officer.   After the war he removed into what is known in the lower part of the State as " The Fork," that is, that portion of the country between the two branches of the Nanticoke.   This tract is altogether in Maryland, but lies adjacent to our State line.   Here Lieutenant Colonel Vaughan died, but when, is not known.   From his living there, the presumption is that he was a farmer ; but this is only inference.   These facts were communicated to me by Hon. John W. Houston, and J. R Elligood, being all that they have ever been able to collect in relation to this gallant officer.

John Patten was a farmer, near Dover.   He was appointed a Lieutenant in Haslet's Regiment, and in September 1776, when Congress called for troops to serve during the war, and fixed our quota at a regiment, or battalion as they called it, he raised a company, was made its captain, and his company was the first to join the regiment, and thus he became *senior* Captain.   Upon their order to the South, Major Vaughan was promoted to the Lieutenant Colonelcy.   Captain Patten, by virtue of his seniority among the captains, was promoted to be Major, and with Vaughan, was taken prisoner at Camden, and being parolled, but not exchanged, did not afterward join his regiment. He was a gallant, brave officer ; indeed, his and Vaughan's capture shows that on that morning they were in their right place—at the head of their regiment. He was with Haslet's regiment in the Battle of Brooklyn and White Plains, and fought with Hall's bravely at Brandywine, Germantown, and Monmouth. He returned to his farm after his parole, and upon the adoption of the United States Constitution, was elected to the Third Congress, as representative from this State. His seat, however, having been contested by Henry Latimer, he was unseated, but was subsequently elected to the Fourth Congress. His son, Joseph Patten, is now a resident of Wilmington, and his daughter having married the late John Wales, Esq., his grand-children by that marriage are also among our most respected citizens.

Robert Kirkwood was born in Mill Creek Hundred, on the farm lately held by the heirs of Andrew Gray, Esq., near to White Clay Creek Church. His sister having married and settled in Newark, he was living with her at the outbreak of the Revolution, and was engaged in mercantile pursuits He obtained a lieutenancy in Haslet's regiment, was with it at Brooklyn and White Plains, and like most of Haslet's officers sought and obtained positions in the new regiment to be raised under the call of September 1776, for men to serve during the war. His company was the second one to join the regiment, Patten's as we have seen, being the first. Patten's commission as Captain is dated November 30th, and Kirkwood's, December 1st, 1776 ; only one day's difference. The officers of Haslet's regiment who joined Hall's, did not participate in the Battle of Trenton and Princeton ; they had been permitted to come home in October and November to recruit for what Congress then greatly wanted—men to serve during the war ; and Hall's regiment was not fully organized at the date of these battles—in fact it did not join the army until the month of April, 1777. Hall's commission as Colonel, is dated April 5th, 1777.

Kirkwood was with his Regiment at Brandywine, German-

town, Monmouth, went south with it, and upon the capture of
Vaughan and Patten, succeeded to the command, by virtue of
his being Senior Captain, after Patten's promotion as Major—
of what was left of it after Camden.

On that day, as we have seen, Maryland and Delaware by
their noble stand, saved whatever there was of honor, but it
was at the cost of their almost entire annihilation. Kirkwood
gathered them up, man by man, as they came into Salisbury
and Hillsborough, and they were constituted into his famous
Light Infantry Company, and were in all the battles afterward, from Cowpens to Eutaw. Whether it was Greene, or
Morgan, or Williams, or Howard, or Lee, speaking in general
order, in letter, or in private conversation, it was always " The
Brave Kirkwood and his Delawares," or " Kirkwood and his
brave Delawares." Is any higher eulogium possible ? Greene, by
odds, the *general* of the revolution—*its soldier*—praise from
him—the others, their fellow soldiers, the officers under whose
eyes, and by whose orders they gave the enemy the *Bayonet*,
—praise from them—it must have been deserved. To show what
Lee thought of Kirkwood, let me read what he says in his memoirs ; in speaking of the battle of Camden, and of the Delaware Regiment being placed, after the capture of Vaughan and
Patten, under Kirkwood's command as Senior Captain.

" The State of Delaware furnished one regiment only, and certainly no
regiment in the army surpassed it in soldiership. The remnant of that
corps, less than two companies, from the battle of Camden, was commanded
by Captain Kirkwood, who passed through the war with high reputation ;
and yet as the line of Delaware consisted but of one regiment, and that regiment was reduced to a Captain's command—Kirkwood never could be promoted in regular routine,—a very glaring defect in the organization of the
army, as it gave advantages to parts of the same armies, denied to other
portions of it. The sequel is singularly hard. Kirkwood retired, upon peace,
as a Captain, and when the army under St. Clair was raised to defend the
West from the Indian Enemy, this veteran resumed his sword as the oldest
Captain of the oldest regiment. In the decisive defeat of the 4th of November, the gallant Kirkwood fell, bravely sustaining his point of the action. It
was the thirty-third time he had risked his life for his country, and he died,
as he had lived, the brave, meritorious, unrewarded Kirkwood."

Virginia alone recognized and appreciated his services. She, by a grant made in 1787, gave him two thousand acres of lands in the North-west territory, which are still held by his grand children, the land being in what is now the State of Ohio. His fate was peculiarly hard and unfortunate ; he passed through thirty-two battles and skirmishes in the revolution, and by great good fortune safely—never even seriously wounded, but in this defeat of St. Clair, a relatively small Indian fight, he was killed. St. Clair, the most unfortunate of all of our revolutionary Generals, was led into ambush by the Indians, and his whole command slaughtered.*

I distinctly recollect two of the officers of this regiment, Major Bennett, and Major Jacquett.

Major Bennett, a tall, spare, old man, wearing knee breeches, is very distinct in my memory. He lived in the house(in Wilmington) now occupied by Dr. Kane, and could be seen any summer afternoon, sitting upon his front pavement, engaged in what we boys did not think a very manly employment, knitting yarn or cotton stockings, but yet, as a Revolutionary hero, was looked at with a sort of awe. He was elected Governor of this State in 1832, but did not live out his term of office, dying in 1836.†

Major Peter Jacquett was a small, thick set man. His family were quite large landholders in New Castle Hundred. After the war he settled on his farm at the end of the causeway, on the road from Wilmington to New Castle, and lived there till his death in 1834. He and Bennett, unlike soldiers generally, were not friends ; they had not spoken to each other for years prior to Jacquett's death. From what I have heard of Jacquett, it was a hard matter for any one to keep on speaking terms with him. He was a cross, morose, quar-

---

* Kirkwood married a Miss England, of White Clay Creek Hundred, in New Castle County. He left two children—a son and daughter—Joseph, the son, removed to Ohio—where a large family survive him. Mary, the daughter, married Arthur Whiteley, of Dorchester County, Maryland, and died in 1850, leaving two children— Gen. R. H. K. Whiteley, of the Army, and Mrs. Mary A. Martin, of Newark.

† He had three children—the late Captain Charles W. Bennett, of the U. S. R. M., and two daughters, Mrs. Lyell and Mrs. Pardee.

relsome man. Upon one occasion, having lost some wheat, he, without cause, accused a neighbor, a very respectable man, a Mr. Thomas Tatlow, of stealing it, and wherever he went he was open and loud in his assertion that "Tom Tatlow was a thief." Tatlow sued him for slander, and recovered quite a heavy verdict. The late Judge Booth, who was his counsel, in explaining to him his liability for his charge against Tatlow, told him that certain language was actionable in itself, that is, if he called Tatlow a thief, or charged him with any other felony, Tatlow could recover without showing any special damage, but that there were certain names which he could call him, without rendering himself liable to damages, unless Tatlow could show special damage. This explanation of the Judge, was the old soldier's chance. He persuaded the Judge to put these words on paper, and wherever and whenever he afterward met Tatlow, he would out with his paper, and beginning at the first would go through the roll of names, so long as Tatlow remained in earshot.

The inscription upon his tomb in the Old Swede's Church, in Wilmington, states :

"That he was born April 6th, 1754, and died upon his farm at Crane Hook, September 13, 1834, aged 80 years.

"That he joined the Delaware Regiment, January 4th, 1776, and was in every general engagement under Washington which took place in Delaware, Pennsylvania, New Jersey, New York and the Eastern States ; was ordered South to the Southern army under Gates, and with the brave De Kalb was in the battle of Camden, where the Delaware Regiment of eight Companies was reduced to two, of ninety-six men each, and when the command devolved on Kirkwood and himself as oldest Captains. Was in the battles of Guilford, second battle of Camden, seige of '96, and battle of the village of that name ; battle of Eutaw Springs, and in every other battle under Greene, until the capture of Cornwallis at Yorktown."

This is a little too strongly and freely drawn, but is, in the main, true. Major Jacquett left no children.

Edward Roche, died within my memory. He was a small man, living in Seventh Street, following the occupation of a Scrivener, and dying in the year 1833.

Capt. John Corse was from Smyrna.

Lieutenant William McKennan was from Christiana Hundred. His father was a clergyman, and preached at what is yet called McKennan's Meeting House.

Lieutenant Stephen McWilliam was from New Castle. However, of them little information has been obtained, and so of Gilder, Purvis, Learmonth, Wilson, Rhodes, and Cox as one hundred years have played sad havoc with every thing connected with them but their reputation. In the case of most of them, their names are not now found among us, and all we can do is to honor and praise them as soldiers.

In speaking of the officers of the line, the staff must not be overlooked. We furnished two surgeons of distinction, Drs. Latimer and Tilton.

Dr. Henry Latimer was born in Newport, in 1752. He commenced the study of medicine in Philadelphia, and completed it by graduating at the Medical College of Edinburgh. Upon his return home he commenced the practice of his profession in Wilmington, but in 1777 he, as well as Dr. Tilton, were appointed Surgeons in the Continental Army, and were attached to what was called the Flying Hospital, and were with the army in all the battles in the Northern Department, from Brandywine to Yorktown. He acquired quite a distinction as a surgeon, and on Peace he returned to the practice of his profession. He was elected a member of our Legislature, after our State organization ; also to Congress from 1793 to 1795, and was elected in 1794 by the Legislature one of the Senators from this State in Congress, and served out his constitutional term. He died in 1819. Mr. Read states, in his life of his father, that Dr. Latimer was the Surgeon of the Delaware Regiment : this is a mistake ; he was attached to no particular regiment. Henry Latimer, Esq., of Wilmington, is his son.

Dr. James Tilton's history is about the same as Dr. Latimer's. He entered the army as Surgeon of Colonel Haslet's Regiment. He was also skilled and honored as a surgeon. Upon the return of Peace he settled on the property now owned by William Howland ; was Surgeon-General of the army in the war of 1812, and died in 1818.

I regret that my information is so meagre as to the officers of the regiment, none at all in fact as to some of them. I have done, however, the best possible under the circumstances. The great lapse of time, the change and removal of their families, the seeming negligence, both upon the part of the State and of their descendants, in the preservation of papers relating to them, prevent at this time almost any accurate record. But their deeds, their sufferings, their valor, should never be forgotten. It was more to be a soldier in those days, than it is now. The improvement in arms of all kinds—the increased range of our modern guns, better ammunition, everything which war requires, has been so improved that the soldier of 1875, scarcely appreciates the difficulties of the soldier of 1775. What would our people now think of the only Commissary Department of an army being the corn fields and orchards on its line of march, and yet this was the case with our own and the Maryland Regiments upon their march to the South. And that was not all ; of clothing they were equally destitute, and yet these men crossed bayonets almost daily with the bravest of England's veterans.

Ramsey, in his history of the United States, vol. 1, p. 209, says :

"The Delaware Regiment was reckoned the most efficient in the Continental Army. It went into active service soon after the commencement of the contest with Great Britain, and served through the whole of it. Courting danger wherever it was to be encountered, frequently forming part of a victorious army, but oftener the companions of their countrymen in the gloom of disaster, the Delawares fought at Brooklyn, at Trenton and at Princeton, at Brandywine and at Germantown, at Guilford and at Eutaw, until at length reduced to a handful of brave men, they concluded their services with the war in the glorious termination of the Southern campaign."

And I conclude this feeble tribute to their memory by saying they were indeed

> "Chiefs graced with scars, and prodigal of blood,
> Stern warriors who for sacred freedom stood."

ADDENDA.

————:o:————

A.

Captain Allen McLane, the father of the late Hon. Louis McLane and Dr. Allen McLane, early in the war, enlisted a partisan company, and served faithfully and bravely through-out the war. He was in most if not all the battles in the Northern Department, and in the battle of Yorktown.

I subjoin a roll of his company for the months of March, April and May, 1779.

Captain Allen McLane's partisan Company of foot, in the service of the United States, taken for the months of March, April, May and June, 1779.

Captain, Allen McLane, commissioned January 13, 1777.
First Lieutenant, A. M. Dunn, commissioned January 13, 1777.
Second Lieutenant, Wm. Jones,   "   "   "   "   killed at Wyoming, April 17, 1779.

First Sergeant, John Edenfield.   Third Sergeant, George Rowan.
Second Sergeant, John Hegan.   Fourth Sergeant, Robert Farrell.
First Corporal, Matthew Cusick,   Second Corporal, John Vandegrift.
Drummer, Philip Wheylon.   Fifer, Eliazer Crane.

Privates.

James Burk,   John Rowles,
Lidford Berry,   William Stratton,
Edward Hines,   Robert Soloway,
Thomas Finn,   Perry Scott,
Thomas Wells,   Charles McMunigill,

4

Thomas Parker,
Barret Alley,
Francis Bilstone,
Ezekiel Clark,
Lazarus Carmedy,

James Longo,
Henry Harneyman,
Moses McLane,
Patrick Dagney,
John Butcher.

B.

To show what were the privations of the soldiers of that day, I subjoin an address from the officers of Hall's Regiment to the General Assembly, on December 4th, 1779.

Address from the Officers of the Delaware Regiment, to the Honorable, the Representatives in the General House of Assembly, of the Delaware State, now sitting in Wilmington, December 4th, 1779.

We, the Officers of the Delaware Regiment, do, in the most grateful manner, thank the Honorable, the House of Assembly, for the two generous Resolves they were pleased to pass in our favor. But whilst we thus express our gratitude, we cannot but complain, that through some defect in the Resolves, or neglect in those who were intrusted with the execution of them, we find our situation little better than it was before they were passed. We have yet received but two month's of the supplies allowed, and have no prospect of receiving any more, as Colonel Craighead informs the Commanding Officer in a letter, dated October 7th, '79, that he has received but 1400 pounds to purchase a quarterly supply of necessaries, that it is inadequate to the purpose, and therefore desires we will each take a dividend of that money in lieu of the necessaries which we are entitled to receive from him, by the Resolve of the Honorable House. This desire we must refuse to comply with, for we cannot conceive that the Honorable House would wish we should compound with Colonel Craighead, and accept one-third of the value, instead of the articles; as this would, in a very great measure, deprive us of the benefit of the Resolve, and again subject us to suffer by the depreciation of our currency, which evil their Resolve was generously intended to prevent.

We further beg leave to acquaint the Honorable House that of the suit of clothes, which they have ordered us to be supplied with, though the season is so far advanced, none of us have received a full suit, some, not one article, and in general, we want many things that are difficult to obtain, and cannot be dispensed with at this season, but at the risk of our health.

We would also beg leave to represent to the Honorable House, how necessary a part of an Officer's dress a hat is, and that we imagine a mistake only was the cause of its not being enumerated among the other articles of clothing, and, therefore, hope they will be pleased to allow us that useful article. We also hope the Honorable House will continue their bounty by allowing us a suit of clothes yearly, at least whilst the currency remains depreciated.

Laboring under many difficulties which the distance from our respective homes, and the general depreciation of the money had thrown upon us, we were once before obliged to make application to the Honorable House for their assistance in removing or alleviating them. The spirit of generosity shown in their resolves on that occasion, encourages us to submit this to their consideration, confident that the welfare and honor of the Regiment, that claims this patronage, are next to the happiness of their country, their greatest wish, and that upon this representation of our case, they will minutely enquire, from what cause their resolves have not been executed, and make such provision for their execution, as will in future prevent applications of this kind from their

Very humble servants,

C. P. BENNETT, L. D.,	PETER JACQUETT, Capt. D. R.
EDWARD ROCHE, Lieut. and P. M.	J. LEARMONTH, Capt. D. R.
THOS. ANDERSON, Lieut. and Q. M.	JOHN WILSON, Capt. D. R.
R. GILDER, Surgeon.	DANIEL P. COX, Lieut.
JOHN PLATT, S. Mate.	HENRY DUFF, Lieut.
J. VAUGHAN, M. D. R.	E. SKILLINGTON, Lieut.
ROBERT KIRKWOOD, C. D. R.	CHAS. KIDD, Lieut.
JOHN CORSE, Lt. D. R.	STEPHEN McWILLIAMS, Ensign D. R.

C.

The tradition in the State is, that our soldiers received the name of "Blue Hen's Chickens," from the fact that a Captain Caldwell took with his company, game chickens, which were from the brood of a blue hen, celebrated in Kent County for their fighting qualities ; and that the officers and men of this company, when not fighting the enemy, amused themselves fighting chickens.

There were two Captain Caldwells, Captain Joseph Caldwell, of Colonel Patterson's Regiment (Flying Camp,) and Captain Jonathan Caldwell, of Colonel Haslet's Regiment.

From the best evidence which I have been able to obtain, it was from Captain Jonathan Caldwell and his company, that our soldiers derived the name. I, therefore, in honor of the brave Captain, his officers and men, add a roll of the company.

Captain Jonathan Caldwell's Company in Col. Haslet's Regiment.

Captain, JONATHAN CALDWELL.
First Lieutenant, JOHN PATTEN.
Second Lieutenant, GEORGE McCALL.
Ensign, JAMES STEVENS.

First Sergeant, John Depoister.
Second Sergeant, Joseph Campbell.
Third Sergeant, John Rowan.
Fourth Sergeant, John Corse.
First Corporal, John McCannon.
Second Corporal, John Dewees.
Third Corporal, Robert Oram.
Fourth Corporal, Isaac Matthews.
Drummer, Robert Thompson.
Fifer, Cornelius Comegys.

Privates.

John Shearn,	John Hart,
James Millington,	Francis Blair,
John Manning,	John Wilson,
John Kinnamon,	John May,
Michael McGinnis,	Thomas Finn,
Robert Solway,	George Riall,
William Plowman,	Peter Grewell,
John Allen,	William Perry,
John Butler,	Ephriam Townsend,
Jacob Wilson,	Isaac Cox,
Nathan Bowen,	John Matthews,
John Pegg,	William Hall,
George Bateman,	Mark Ivans,
Joseph Robinson.	Hosea Wilson,
James Carson,	John Edingfield,
John Nickerson,	Nathan Gaus,

John Spring,
Zachariah Baily,
Peter Bice,
'James Robinson,
John Simmons,
Robert Graham,
John Kelly,
Allen Robinett,
William Edingfield,
Robert Ferrell,

Lewis Humphreys,
Kimber Haslet,
Garrett Fagan,
Harman Clarke,
John Tims,
Lambert Williams,
William Mott,
Alexander McDowell,
Daniel Lawley,
Peter Wilcox.